Traveling Through Time

SHIPS

NEIL MORRIS

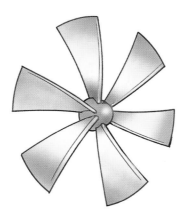

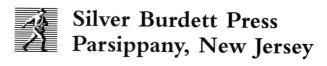

Silver Burdett Press

Parsippany, New Jersey

TRAVELING THROUGH TIME

SHIPS

First published in the U.K. in 1997 by
Belitha Press Limited,
London House, Great Eastern Wharf,
Parkgate Road, London SW11 4NQ

Editor: Jinny Johnson
Designer: Guy Callaby
Picture researcher: Juliet Duff

First published in the United States in 1998 by
Silver Burdett Press
A Division of Simon & Schuster
299 Jefferson Road
Parsippany, New Jersey 07054

Library of Congress Cataloging-in-Publication Data
Morris, Neil, 1946-
Traveling through time, ships/Neil Morris.
p. cm.
Includes index.
Summary: Surveys the history of ships and their uses, from the first sailing ships
to the ocean liners of today.
1. Ships—History—Juvenile literature. [1. Ships—History.] I. Title. II. Series:
Morris, Neil, 1946- Traveling through time.
VM150.M67   1997   97-12533
387—dc21   CIP   AC
ISBN 0-382-39789-4 (LSB)   10 9 8 7 6 5 4 3 2 1
ISBN 0-382-39790-8 (PBK)   10 9 8 7 6 5 4 3 2 1

Printed in Hong Kong

Words in **bold** appear in the glossary on pages 30–31.

Picture acknowledgments:
t=top; b=bottom; c=center; r=right l=left

AA & A: 16 both
J. Allan Cash: 28c
Bridgeman Art Library: 17
Mary Evans Picture Library: 13r, 25l
Robert Harding Picture Library 8l, 9, 12t, 13l, 20t
Michael Holford: 8r, 21
Hulton Getty Picture Collection: 12b
Peter Newark's Pictures: 20b, 24t
Fred Olsen Travel: 29t
Princess Cruises: 28–29b
Quadrant Picture Library: 28t
Retrograph Archive Ltd: 4–5t, 24b
Stena Line: 5b
Tony Stone Worldwide: 4b, 25r

Front cover and main artworks by Terry Hadler
All other artworks by Graham Rosewarne

Contents

Introduction

What is the difference between a ship and a boat? A ship is a large vessel that can sail the world's oceans, while a boat is smaller and makes shorter voyages on seas, rivers, and lakes. Ships are the oldest form of long-distance transportation. They have carried people and goods across the seas for at least 5,000 years. During that time people have traveled in ships to explore and discover new lands, to settle in new parts of the world, to trade with others, and to conquer new territory.

► Passengers enjoying fun and games on the sports deck of a 1920s ocean liner.

4

Sailing ships

Early boats and ships were rowed with oars and paddles. Sails first appeared on ancient Egyptian ships, and the power of the wind to push a ship along was used right through to the nineteenth century. The first boats were made of reeds, and then planks of wood. Over thousands of years, wooden ships got bigger and so needed more and better sails. Shipbuilders gradually improved the arrangement of ships' **masts** and sails. They reached their highest point in the mid-1800s with the fast sailing **clippers**. Sailing ships are still used today, especially for sports and leisure, and there are even round-the-world yacht races.

◄ Chinese **junks** are still used as working ships. This one is carrying tourists around Hong Kong harbor.

Engine power

The steam engine eventually took over from the power of human muscles and the wind to propel ships along. The first **steamships** of the nineteenth century were not as reliable or even as fast as sailing ships. But engineers and shipbuilders soon improved the steamers and then began to make ships of iron instead of wood. Iron ships were stronger and could hold more passengers and cargo. For a hundred years, from about 1850, ocean liners carried millions of passengers around the world.

Changing times

Since 1950 ocean liners and other ships have had to compete with the jet airplane. On speed and cost jets have won the competition easily. However, luxury ships are still used for vacation cruises, smaller ships operate as **ferries** for cars and passengers, and big cargo ships are as busy as ever. More recently, the success of high-speed passenger ferries has shown that many people still want to travel by ship.

5

▶ Modern ports are designed to make the loading of cars and passengers onto high-speed ferries as easy as possible.

Trading
by sea

During ancient times people became
rich and powerful by controlling the
seas. Ships were used both to explore new
territory across the seas and to trade with
other lands. They were also important
during wartime, carrying soldiers and
weapons to enemy shores.

A Roman **merchant ship**, such as this one dating from around A.D. 200, was used to carry a wide range of **cargo**. It was up to 180 feet long and had two sails, a **mainsail** in the middle and a **spritsail** at the **bow**. The oars at the **stern** were for steering. The carved swan's head represented the Egyptian goddess Isis, the sailors' guardian.

Ancient sailors

The ancient Egyptians made their first boats out of bundles of reeds. By about 3000 B.C., they had discovered that boats could be moved along by sails that caught the wind. A few hundred years later, the Egyptians started making ships out of short planks of wood. Some of these ships were more than 100 feet long. The Phoenicians, who lived on the eastern Mediterranean coast, built larger cargo ships from giant cedar planks. They also built narrower, faster fighting ships. The ancient Greeks used a similar design, and by 300 B.C. some of their biggest ships had four sails.

Roman merchant ships

The Romans sailed ships similar to those of the ancient Greeks, and they built up the largest fleet of ancient times. Their biggest merchant ships could carry hundreds of tons of grain from Egypt, to feed the Roman people. At that time there were no passenger ships, so travelers had to sail on merchant craft. There were cabins in the stern of the ship, though these were often full of prisoners or slaves, forced to live in cramped conditions.

Beyond the Mediterranean

The earliest Egyptian boats were built to travel on the Nile River. But about 3,500 years ago, Egyptians carried shipbuilding materials across the desert from the Nile to the Red Sea. Then they set sail for a land they called Punt, in East Africa. Centuries later the Phoenicians sailed through the Strait of Gibraltar and traveled to West Africa and Britain, where they bought tin from Cornish mines. In about 330 B.C. a Greek astronomer named Pytheas even sailed as far north as the Arctic Circle, to a land he called Thule. This may have been the coast of Norway or Iceland.

▼ In 1954 an Egyptian archaeologist discovered a stone-covered pit beside the Great Pyramid at Giza. When the stones were removed, the pit was found to contain this wooden boat. It had been partly taken apart because it was too long for the pit. The boat may have been used to carry King Khufu's body across the Nile to the Great Pyramid, in about 2580 B.C.

8

▲ Much can be learned about early boats and sailing methods from ancient pictures. This wall painting was discovered in an ancient Egyptian tomb. It shows Sennefer, mayor of Thebes, and his wife sailing on the Nile River, around 1450 B.C. Thebes, an ancient city on the Nile, was once capital of Egypt. The boat was built from bundles of papyrus reeds, which grew along the banks of the Nile.

▼ About 3,000 years ago, the Phoenicians were the greatest sailors of the Mediterranean Sea. Their cedar-wood ships were strong, powered by oars and a single sail. The Phoenicians sailed from their cities of Tyre and Sidon, in modern Lebanon. About 814 B.C. they founded the city of Carthage on the northern coast of Africa.

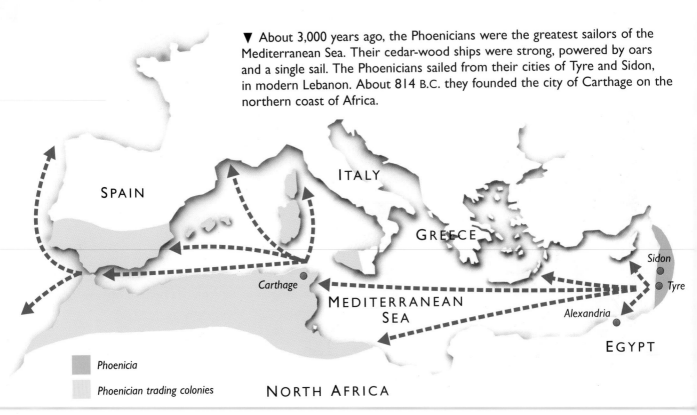

SPAIN

ITALY

GREECE

Sidon

Carthage

Tyre

MEDITERRANEAN SEA

Alexandria

EGYPT

Phoenicia

Phoenician trading colonies

NORTH AFRICA

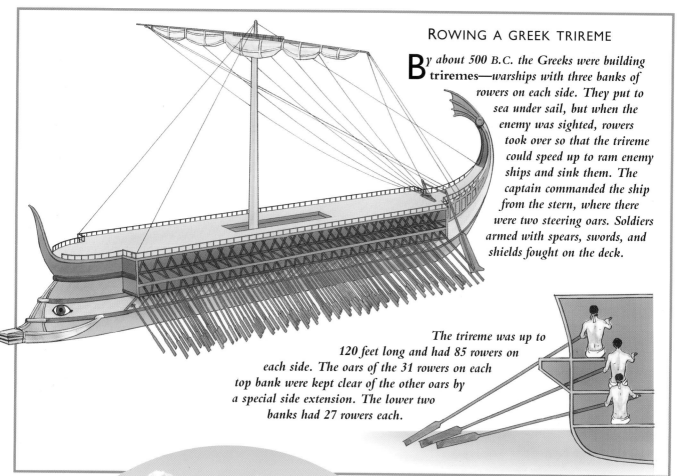

ROWING A GREEK TRIREME

*B*y about 500 B.C. the Greeks were building triremes—warships with three banks of rowers on each side. They put to sea under sail, but when the enemy was sighted, rowers took over so that the trireme could speed up to ram enemy ships and sink them. The captain commanded the ship from the stern, where there were two steering oars. Soldiers armed with spears, swords, and shields fought on the deck.

The trireme was up to 120 feet long and had 85 rowers on each side. The oars of the 31 rowers on each top bank were kept clear of the other oars by a special side extension. The lower two banks had 27 rowers each.

9

◀ Traditionally the Aymara people live by fishing in Lake Titicaca, which lies on the border between Peru and Bolivia in South America. They also farm around the shores of the lake. The Aymara still travel and fish using boats made from the local reeds, as their ancestors have done for centuries. The reed boats of the Aymaras do the same job as those built by the Egyptians thousands of years ago.

The climate here is harsh, since Lake Titicaca lies in the Andes Mountains, 12,500 feet above sea level. This is the highest lake in the world that is big enough for boats to sail on.

Crossing oceans

Nobody knows exactly when people first sailed across the world's two biggest oceans, the Pacific and the Atlantic. But it is certain that they traveled in a variety of craft, from simple rafts to sleek **longships**.

A Viking longship was steered with a broad oar on the right-hand side of the stern. The word **starboard**, meaning a ship's right-hand side, comes from this. The ship was about 80 feet long, and its single sail was made of a tough woolen cloth strengthened by strips of leather.

Canoes and rafts

Polynesia is made up of a large group of islands in the Pacific Ocean. Most experts believe that the original Polynesians crossed the ocean from Southeast Asia, between 1,000 and 3,000 years ago. They traveled in large canoes, using sails and paddles. People from South America may also have sailed more than 3,800 miles in balsa-wood rafts to found colonies in Polynesia.

Longships and traders

In ancient times the people of Scandinavia—now Norway, Sweden, and Denmark—built canoes, and boats made of animal hides. These gradually developed into the ships for which Scandinavians are most famous, Viking longships. Between the late 700s and 1100, these were the best European ships. Many were used as warships, to raid other lands. They had up to 30 oars on each side, which were used near land, when extra speed was needed, or when there was little wind. On the open sea, the single sail was generally used.

Viking voyages

A Viking called Erik the Red sailed his longship from Iceland to Greenland in the tenth century. His son, Leif Eriksson, traveled even farther west about the year 1000. Eriksson named the first land he reached Helluland, meaning "land of flat stones." This was probably present-day Baffin Island, in Canada. The explorers then sailed on to Markland ("forest land"), which was probably the Canadian mainland of Labrador. And finally they reached Vinland ("wine land"), where wild grapes grew. This must have been somewhere in the northeastern United States or northeastern Canada. This great voyage took place nearly 500 years before Christopher Columbus crossed the Atlantic.

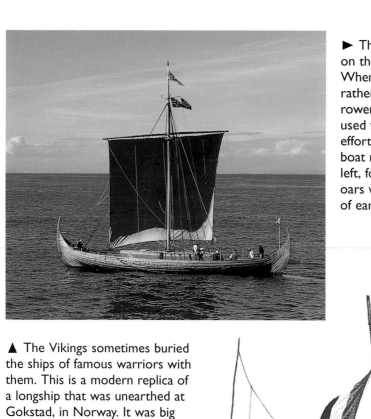

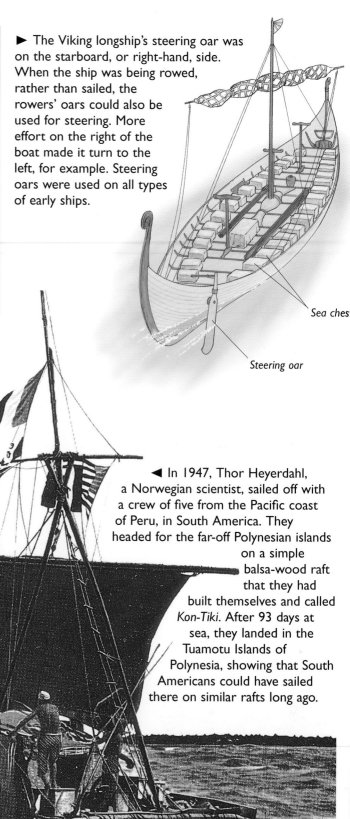

► The Viking longship's steering oar was on the starboard, or right-hand, side. When the ship was being rowed, rather than sailed, the rowers' oars could also be used for steering. More effort on the right of the boat made it turn to the left, for example. Steering oars were used on all types of early ships.

Sea ches[

Steering oar

▲ The Vikings sometimes buried the ships of famous warriors with them. This is a modern replica of a longship that was unearthed at Gokstad, in Norway. It was big enough for 16 rowers on each side, who used their sea chests as rowing benches. Because they were light and had shallow bottoms, longships could also be rowed up rivers and then carried overland to another river or coast.

12

◄ In 1947, Thor Heyerdahl, a Norwegian scientist, sailed off with a crew of five from the Pacific coast of Peru, in South America. They headed for the far-off Polynesian islands on a simple balsa-wood raft that they had built themselves and called *Kon-Tiki*. After 93 days at sea, they landed in the Tuamotu Islands of Polynesia, showing that South Americans could have sailed there on similar rafts long ago.

▼ This ship, sailing in the Indian Ocean off the coast of Kenya, is called a dhow. Originally Arab ships, dhows have been sailed for many centuries in the Persian Gulf and the Red Sea, as well as in the Indian Ocean. Arabs sailed to the Kenyan coast and settled there in the seventh century.

The triangular-shaped sail is called a **lateen**. The lateen sail was the forerunner of almost every kind of modern sail, including those used in yachts. The wind blows around the sail, which is set along the length of the ship rather than across it. This makes it easier to sail, even when the wind is not directly behind the ship.

▲ This early twentieth-century illustration shows a large expedition of Solomon Islanders putting out to sea. The Solomon Islands form part of Melanesia, another of the groups of Pacific islands, along with Polynesia.

Solomon Islanders traditionally went to sea in huge wooden **dugouts**, some of which could hold as many as a hundred people. These big canoes were often beautifully carved. Today they are mostly used for special ceremonies.

13

CLINKER AND CARVEL

*V*iking longships were **clinker-built,** *which means that the bottom edge of one plank overlapped the top edge of the one below. Many small boats are still built that way today. Roman and earlier ships were* **carvel-built,** *with the planks placed edge to edge to give a smooth surface. Many later ships were also carvel-built.*

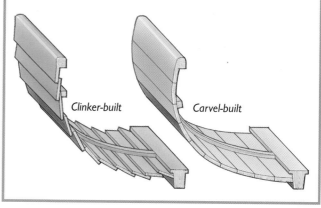

Clinker-built   Carvel-built

To the
New World

By about 1250, shipbuilders in Europe had developed a sturdy trading ship. It had a wide hull that could hold bulky cargoes, one large square sail, structures called **castles** at the **prow** and the stern, and a new method of steering, called a **rudder**.

The *Mayflower* was an ordinary small merchant ship, about 90 feet long and 25 feet wide. As well as three masts, it had a **bowsprit** pointing forward from the prow, giving it a total of six sails. There was a high **sterncastle**, or **poop deck**, at the rear of the ship.

Full rigging

By about 1450, Mediterranean shipbuilders had added more sails to their trading ships. The new, **full-rigged** ship had a **mainmast** in the middle, a foremast in the forward part, and a **mizzenmast** at the back. The mainmast and foremast each carried two square sails, and the mizzenmast had a triangular sail. The full **rigging** made the ships faster, and the hinged rudder at the stern gave much better steering. The explorers Christopher Columbus, Vasco da Gama, and Ferdinand Magellan all sailed in full-rigged ships.

From Plymouth to Plymouth

The full-rigged *Mayflower* set sail from Plymouth, England, on September 16, 1620. On board were 102 men, women, and children. They included the Pilgrim Fathers, who were looking for a new life in the New World and freedom to worship God in their own way. The *Mayflower* crossed the Atlantic Ocean during its stormiest season, and the voyage lasted over nine weeks. The Pilgrims reached land where the state of Massachusetts is today and named their settlement Plymouth.

Life on board

Conditions must have been hard and cramped on the *Mayflower*, which had a crew of 28 men under Captain Christopher Jones. The passengers ate the same food day after day—biscuits, salted meat, dried fish, and cheese, washed down with beer. The seas were very rough for such a small ship, and some of the passengers were seasick for weeks on end.

INSIDE THE *MAYFLOWER*

1 Forecastle, where ordinary sailors slept and the cook made meals for the crew.
2 Windlass, a machine for raising anchor.
3 Hold, the main cargo area.
4 Capstan, a pulley used to raise cargo.
5 Steerage, a cabin for the ship's officers.

6 Whipstaff, a lever connected to the rudder, moved by the helmsman according to orders shouted from above.
7 Roundhouse, or chart room.
8 Great cabin, for the captain.
9 'Tween decks, where passengers lived.
10 Gun room, where two cannons were kept in case of attack.

▲ This thirteenth-century trading ship was called a **cog**. The small **forecastle** at the front of the ship served as a platform from which soldiers could fire arrows in times of trouble. And the larger sterncastle gave some shelter to passengers and crew. Cogs had a large hinged rudder in the middle of the stern, which was far more effective than the earlier steering oar.

▼ A modern replica of Christopher Columbus's full-rigged ship, the *Santa Maria*, anchored in Barcelona harbor in Spain. This was the largest of the three ships that sailed on Columbus's first voyage to the New World, but space on board was still limited for the crew of 40 men. Columbus had his own cabin with a bunk, but the crew had to sleep in roll-up beds among the cargo, or on deck in good weather.

▼ The *Mayflower*'s voyage of 1620 from Plymouth, Devon, to Plymouth, Massachusetts, was re-enacted over 300 years later. A replica of the ship, called *Mayflower II*, was built in England and sailed to America without engines in 1957. The modern voyage took 55 days, and *Mayflower II* is now a popular floating museum in Massachusetts.

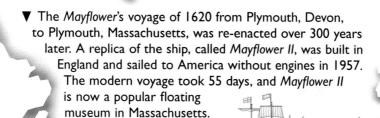

Plymouth, UK

Plymouth, U.S.

Lisbon

Palos

SAN SALVADOR

CANARY ISLANDS

CUBA

17

▲ Christopher Columbus left Palos, in Spain, on August 3, 1492. On October 12 he sighted San Salvador Island. Columbus thought he had found the East Indies, and he called the local islanders "Indians." Near Hispaniola the *Santa Maria* ran aground and was wrecked. Columbus transferred to the *Niña*, and arrived back at Palos on March 15, 1493.

HISPANIOLA

When Columbus sailed west, he was not really sure where he was going. Some of the crew thought they would never see land again, or that they might fall off the edge of the world!

◄ The American clipper ship *Flying Cloud*, built in 1851. Clippers had five or six rows of large sails on three masts, which made them very fast. They were called clippers because their speed allowed them to clip days off the sailing time of other ships. Clippers carried people to California all the way around Cape Horn at the tip of South America, many in search of riches during the gold rush. British clippers sped wool from Australia and tea from China.

Full steam ahead

For thousands of years ships were powered by the wind or by human energy. The invention of the steam engine in the late eighteenth century changed all that. But the first steamships were not all a great success, and they still had sails—just in case the engine broke down!

The *Great Eastern*, launched in 1858, was 692 feet long and 85 feet wide—easily the largest ship built up to that time. It had three forms of power—a **propeller**, sails on six masts, and two **paddle wheels** driven by separate steam engines. The giant paddle wheels were 56 feet in diameter.

Early steamships

The first really successful steamship was built in 1807 by the American engineer Robert Fulton. His *Clermont* steamed for 150 miles up the Hudson River from New York to Albany. Twelve years later the American-built *Savannah* became the first steamship to cross the Atlantic. By 1835 paddle-steamers were making regular transatlantic crossings under steam power alone.

Brunel's steamships

The British engineer Isambard Kingdom Brunel, the famous designer of railway bridges and tunnels, launched the *Great Britain* in 1843. This propeller-driven iron steamship had cabins for 60 first-class passengers and room for 300 more. But Brunel wanted to build a much larger ship. He achieved this with the *Great Eastern*, which was over twice as long and could carry over 4,000 passengers!

Across the Atlantic

The *Great Eastern* was big enough to carry 15,000 tons of coal to fire its boilers. This was enough coal for the ship to steam from Europe to Australia without refueling, but there were not enough passengers every trip to pay for its operating costs. Fortunately the *Great Eastern* found another use. It was the only ship in the world big enough to carry the 2,500 miles of telegraph cable needed to stretch across the Atlantic Ocean floor from Ireland to Canada. The ship's passenger cabins were replaced by cable-winding gear. On the first attempt to lay the cable, in 1865, the cable broke. A year later, efforts were successful and the first transatlantic cable was laid.

Rudder   Propeller   Lifeboat

20

▲ The Mississippi River, which flows from the northern United States to the Gulf of Mexico, is famous for its steamboats. They first steamed out of New Orleans in 1812, powered by the now famous large paddle wheel at the stern. The *Natchez* (above) is a modern example. Tourists can also still travel on the world's largest river boat, the 380-foot-long *Mississippi Queen*.

PROPELLERS

A ship's propeller is connected to a shaft, which is turned by the engine. As it turns, the propeller pushes water backward, and this thrusts the ship forward.

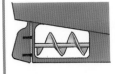

An early screw propeller

Bladed propellers replaced screws. Some had two blades. The Great Eastern's propeller had four.

◄ The first ships passing through the Suez Canal, on November 17, 1869. The canal runs through Egypt to connect the Mediterranean with the Red Sea. Before it opened, ships going from Europe to Asia had to sail around the southern tip of Africa—thousands of miles farther.

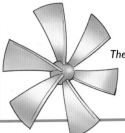

The Great Britain's propeller had six blades.

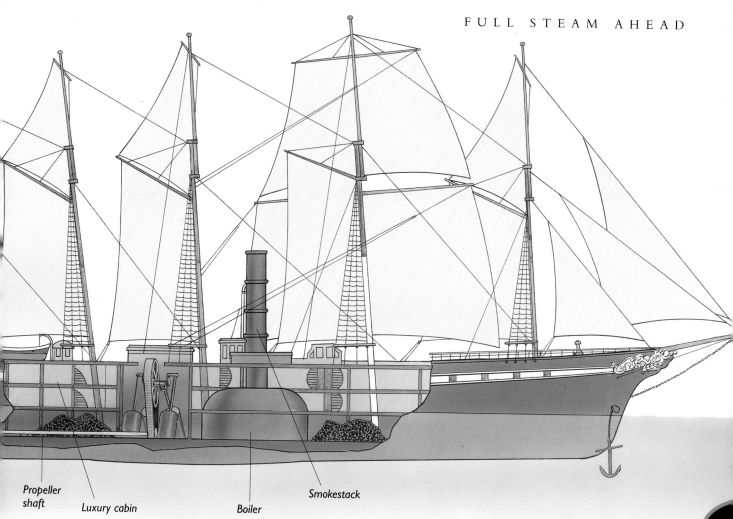

Propeller
shaft
Luxury cabin
Boiler
Smokestack

▲ Some of the working parts of the *Great Britain* are shown above. Fuel was burned to heat water in the boiler, which made steam. The steam pushed **pistons** in the engine, which turned the propeller shaft. The shaft was connected to the propeller, which pushed the ship along. Smoke and extra steam from the boiler came out of the **smokestack**.

Like other early steamships, the *Great Britain* had a full set of sails on six masts. The ship was 320 feet long and 50 feet wide, and in 1845 it became the first propeller-driven ship to cross the Atlantic.

▲ The *Savannah* arriving at Liverpool in 1819, after making the first steam-powered Atlantic crossing. The *Savannah* was a full-rigged sailing ship, with paddle wheels added. During the 29-day Atlantic voyage, the engine ran for a total of 85 hours before using up all its coal and wood fuel.

The Blue Riband

The great ocean liners of the twentieth century were perhaps the most famous and best-loved ships of all time. For many years the liners competed for the Blue Riband, a trophy awarded for the fastest crossing of the Atlantic Ocean.

The *Queen Mary* was 1,017 feet long (half as long again as the *Great Eastern*) and 120 feet wide. It had four propellers, each 20 feet across and weighing 38.5 tons. The liner was launched in September 1934 as an empty shell, then fitted out and tested, ready to make its maiden voyage in May 1936.

Transatlantic trophy

British, French, and German liners were the early holders of the Blue Riband. It took the *Queen Mary* a couple of transatlantic crossings to get up to full speed, but then it took the record. It steamed from New York to Southampton, England in just under four days, at an average speed of 30.6 **knots** (35 miles per hour). Ships' speeds are normally calculated in knots, which are nautical miles per hour. The American liner *United States* broke the record in both directions on its maiden voyage in 1952, with an average of 35.4 knots (41 miles per hour). This is still the record for a passenger liner.

Luxury at sea

Traveling in one of the great ocean liners was a luxurious experience. They were like vast floating hotels, with ballrooms, swimming pools, and sports courts as well as dining rooms and menus to rival the best restaurants. The *Queen Mary* carried 2,000 passengers in three classes—first or cabin class, second or tourist class, and third class. First-class passengers had use of the upper decks, second-class cabins were in the stern, and third class was deep in the **hull**. No other form of transportation has ever been able to compete with the liners' level of luxury and service.

Competing for passengers

During the 1950s and 1960s, ocean liners faced increasing competition from jet aircraft. The planes could not offer the same luxury, but they were much faster! After a thousand Atlantic crossings, the *Queen Mary* was taken out of service in 1967. The liner sailed to Long Beach, California, where it remains as a popular tourist attraction. Its sister ship, *Queen Elizabeth*, was destroyed by fire in 1972.

► An artist's interpretation of the sinking of the *Titanic*, which happened in the early hours of April 15, 1912. At the time the world's largest, fastest and most luxurious ship, the *Titanic* was also thought to be unsinkable. But on its first voyage, it struck an iceberg in the North Atlantic. At first the crew thought that the damage was slight, but about two hours later the ship plunged to the bottom of the ocean and more than 1500 people drowned. There was not enough room for everyone in the lifeboats.

The tragedy of the *Titanic* led to new safety regulations for ships, including a rule that there must be enough lifeboats to carry all passengers and crew.

▼ This 1935 poster advertised the transatlantic service of the French liner *Normandie*, which competed for size, speed, and luxury with the *Queen Mary* and *Queen Elizabeth*. The *Normandie* was destroyed by fire in New York harbor in 1942.

24

CⁱᵉG.ˡᵉ TRANSATLANTIQUE
French Line

NORMANDIE

LONGITUDINAL SECTION
S/S NORMANDIE
79,280 TONS GROSS REGISTERED

▼ The *Queen Elizabeth 2*, known as the *QE2*, was launched in 1967 and carries on the tradition of the great *Queen* liners. It still makes transatlantic crossings, as well as carrying tourists to other parts of the world, such as the Mediterranean and the Caribbean.

The *QE2* is 965 feet long and has a cruising speed of 32.5 knots (37 miles per hour). It carries a crew of 1,000 and more than 1,700 passengers. Different parts of *QE2* are shown in this cutaway illustration.

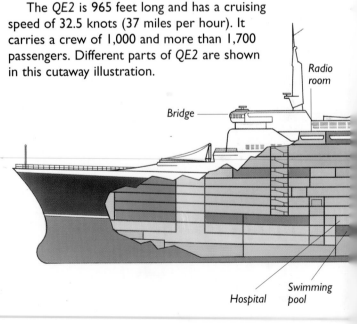

Radio room

Bridge

Hospital

Swimming pool

▼ The *Queen Mary* today, a tourist attraction and luxury hotel at Long Beach, California. The liner arrived here in December 1967, and it took over three years to convert the ship to its new purpose. In order to take out some unwanted machinery, engineers had to remove the ship's famous three smokestacks. When they did so, the smokestacks collapsed—only their 110 coats of paint had held them together! They were later replaced with three new steel smokestacks.

▲ One of the *Queen Mary*'s original **staterooms**, or cabins. Today 365 of the original first-class staterooms have been restored, to make up the Queen Mary Hotel at Long Beach, California. There are shops and restaurants on board, too.

25

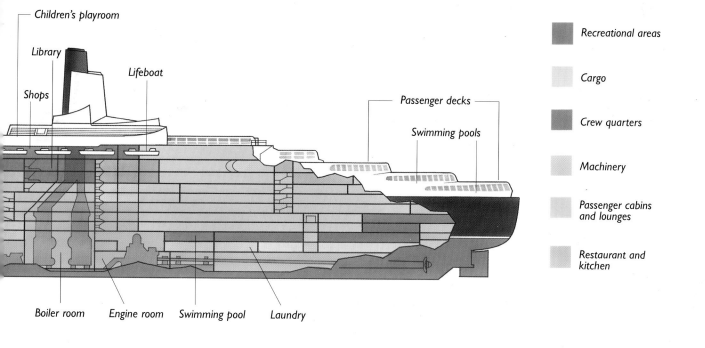

Children's playroom

Library

Shops

Lifeboat

Passenger decks

Swimming pools

Boiler room   Engine room   Swimming pool   Laundry

Recreational areas

Cargo

Crew quarters

Machinery

Passenger cabins and lounges

Restaurant and kitchen

Speeding into

the future

Car and passenger ferries have been part of the world's shipping fleet for a long time. In recent years ferries have become bigger and faster, as they try to compete with planes and even train-tunnels, such as the Channel Tunnel between England and France.

The twin-hulled *Stena Explorer* is an HSS 1500 ferry, meaning a High-speed Sea Service carrying 1,500 passengers. It can also carry 375 cars, or 100 cars and 50 trucks. This huge ferry is 407 feet long and 131 feet wide, with a service speed of 40 knots (46 miles per hour).

High-speed ferries

The new types of fast ferry have twin hulls, which give the ferries the advantage of being both light and stable. They do not roll from side to side as much as single-hulled ships, and so are more comfortable for passengers. HSS ferries are driven by four gas-turbine jet engines, which drive sea water out of the stern of the ship at great pressure. Movable nozzles turn the jets to left and right, and these movements steer the ship. This new technology makes the high-speed ferries over twice as fast as the old, propeller-driven ships.

Cruising along

Today most liners are used for vacation cruises. The *Queen Elizabeth 2* still crosses the Atlantic between Southampton and New York five times a year, and at other times is used for cruises. There are even special holidays for passengers who want to travel one way across the Atlantic on this luxury ship, and back on Concorde, the fastest passenger plane. More adventurous travelers can go on voyages with other shipping lines to visit northern fjords and the Arctic Ocean.

All kinds of crafts

Ferries and cruising ships are popular with travelers and they are becoming bigger, faster, and more comfortable. Cargo ships are in great demand with trading companies all over the world, and today's largest ships are oil tankers. The biggest tanker is 1,500 feet long! As people have more leisure time, boating has become a more popular sport. Some private sailing yachts and motor launches are very large, with expert crews hired by the owners to operate them. Ships have been traveling the world's seas for thousands of years, and new vessels are set to go on doing so in the future.

27

FLYING ACROSS THE WATER

A hydrofoil is a type of boat that can lift itself above the surface of the water when it is traveling at high speeds. It has wings, called foils, beneath the hull, and these act like aircraft wings to push the boat upward. When the hull is above the water, hydrofoils travel faster with the same amount of power. At low speeds hydrofoils float on the water like other craft.

Hull

Foil

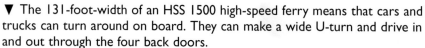

Floating on its hull

Speeding on its foils

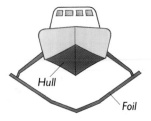

◄ A luxury private cruising ship dwarfs the smaller motor launches beside it. They are all moored in the marina of the Mediterranean port of Monaco, one of the most famous resorts in Europe. This huge ship has a **helipad**, so that the owner can speed to and from the nearest airport by helicopter. Such large ships are extremely expensive both to buy and to run, and owners hire a full crew to look after them.

28

▼ The 131-foot-width of an HSS 1500 high-speed ferry means that cars and trucks can turn around on board. They can make a wide U-turn and drive in and out through the four back doors.

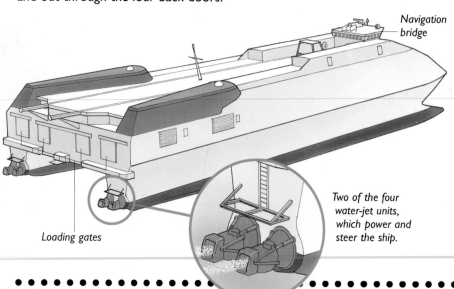

Navigation bridge

Loading gates

Two of the four water-jet units, which power and steer the ship.

▶ *Star Clipper* is a modern clipper ship that carries passengers across the Atlantic Ocean to the Caribbean Sea, and through the Suez Canal and across the Indian Ocean to Thailand and Malaysia. This beautiful ship is 361 feet long and has a sail area of 35,522 square feet. A crew of 72 looks after 170 vacationers. The difference between this and the original clippers is the addition of a diesel engine with a single propeller and up-to-date navigation aids—as well as air conditioning, television, and telephones in the luxurious cabins!

▼ *Sun Princess* went into service in 1996, offering the very latest in luxury Caribbean cruising. This cruise ship is 856 feet long, and can carry 1,950 passengers at a cruising speed of 21 knots (24 miles per hour).

The *Sun Princess, Star Clipper,* and HSS offer three very different, modern ways of traveling by ship.

29

Glossary

bow The front end of a ship.

bowsprit A pole extending forward from the bow of a sailing ship.

cargo Goods carried by ship.

carvel-built Built with the edges of the hull's planks placed next to each other.

castle A raised structure at the front of a ship (the forecastle) or at the back (the sterncastle).

clinker-built Built with the edges of the hull's planks overlapping each other.

clipper A fast sailing ship with many sails that could clip days off the sailing times of other ships.

cog A European merchant ship with a single square sail.

dugout A canoe made by hollowing out a log.

ferry A ship that carries passengers, cars, and goods as a regular service.

forecastle A raised structure at the front of a ship.

foremast The mast nearest the bow.

full-rigged Having three or more masts.

helipad A place where helicopters can land and take off.

hull The main body of a ship.

junk A Chinese sailing ship with square sails supported by bamboo slats.

knot One nautical mile per hour, or 1.15 miles per hour.

lateen sail A large triangular sail set along the length of a ship.

longship A narrow, open Viking ship with oars and a square sail.

mainmast The principal mast of a ship.

mainsail A ship's largest sail, on the mainmast.

mast A tall, upright pole, originally made of wood, for carrying a ship's sails and rigging.

merchant ship A trading ship used for carrying goods.

mizzenmast The mast behind the mainmast, toward the back of a ship.

paddle wheel One of two large wheels at the side of a ship that turn to push it along.

piston A part that slides back and forth in an engine's cylinder and turns the propeller shaft.

poop deck A raised structure at the back of a ship.

propeller A set of blades that turn in the water to push a ship along.

prow The front end of a ship.

rigging The ropes and cables used to control a ship's sails.

rudder A hinged board or plate at the back of a ship that can be turned to change the ship's direction.

smokestack A chimney for carrying away smoke and gases given off by a ship's engine.

spritsail A square sail on the small mast at the front of a ship.

starboard A ship's right-hand side.

stateroom A private luxury cabin in a ship.

steamship A ship powered by a steam engine.

stern The back end of a ship.

sterncastle A raised structure at the back of a ship.

trireme An ancient Greek warship with three banks of rowers on each side.

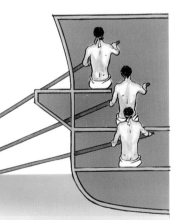

Index